DAGENHAM DAYS

My memories, poems
& tales of mystery

by

Frank Beale

Valence House Publications

Published in 2020 by Valence House Publications
Valence House, Becontree Avenue
Dagenham, Essex RM8 3HT

www.valencehousecollections.co.uk

ISBN 978-1-911391-08-1

Introduction and all editorial material copyright ©Valence House Publications 2020

All rights reserved. No part of this book may be reproduced or transmitted in any form or by any means, electronic or mechanical, including photocopying, recording or by any information storage or retrieval system, without permission from the Publisher in writing

Cover Images : The Dagenham Idol - original on display at Valence House Museum.

Cover Photo - Frank Beale author at Valence House Museum.

All other photos - The photos in this book are either property of Valence House or free to use images from wikimedia commons.

When I was young, I wondered why older people nearly always talked of the past in preference to the present, but now that I have reached that stage classified as older, I understand why.

I think it is because the present is going at a much faster speed than we can keep up with, and new inventions and discoveries keep coming at a rate that we never could have imagined in our younger days.

So, it's easier to remember the past as a more leisurely time, though it probably wasn't as we were living it.

If you are a young person today, please don't mock the old and their memories. Just remember that in as much as today is the foundation of tomorrow, it was yesterday that made today.

These stories and poems are founded on my experiences and imagination and growing older, at last I have found the time to dream a little and reflect on things I have heard and learnt. Tackling modern technology has been a challenge but it has enabled me to release my thoughts. I'm not writing to seek your praise, but if you share a few moments with me perhaps you will be a little amused, intrigued and dare I hope, entertained.

Frank Beale
March 2020

GOOD OLDE DAYS

My first memory was being hit with a spade when I was about six years old, in 1934. I was helping my brothers clear a patch of the garden when my eldest brother, who was wielding the spade, took a sideswipe at a half buried brick and his back swing parted one of my eyebrows. My next, was being held down by what seemed like hundreds of nurses whilst a doctor put in three stitches. Whether the blow killed all previous memory, I will never know, but I do know that very many more memories remain of my life after that.

The winters around 1934 were much colder than they are now and we were without central heating, and had only a small fire in the living room. When we went to bed, we kept our socks on and we put any spare overcoats on the bed to keep warm. A stone hot water bottle was also put in the bed before we went up.

In the mornings, we very often had to scrape ice from the inside of the windows before we could see out, and stepping out of bed, if we stood on lino instead of the rug, we woke up very fast indeed!

Boys wore short trousers whatever the season and our knees and legs used to get very cold. At fourteen years old, boys were bought their first long trouser suit, so that they could go out to look for work.

Coal was the main fuel, with occasional logs to put on after the fire was burning well. Sometimes, people came round the houses, selling 1d bundles of chopped wood to start the fires. The storage cupboard for the coal was in the middle of the house, so when it was time for the coalman to deliver we had to make sure that all the inside doors were closed in an effort to stop the dust that rose up when the coal was tipped from the sacks, getting into any of the rooms. It was never completely successful and it took many hours to clean up, with only a broom and dusters to do the job.

Even worse was the mess when the chimney had to be swept! Even though the chimney sweep put sheets against the fireplace, the soot seemed to seep out and cover everything in the room. The only interesting part was watching for the brush to appear from the top of the chimney pot. Some people 'swept' their chimneys by setting fire to them and putting lighted paper up the chimney to ignite the soot. This often got out of hand and the Fire Brigade had to be called. You always knew when someone was 'sweeping' this way from the black smoke that poured from the chimney. Without vacuum cleaners it was hard work cleaning up, finishing with the lino needing to be scrubbed; a hands and knees job. No fitted carpets in those days, only two or three small rugs around the table that usually stood in the centre of the room. If the chimney caught fire accidentally, we had to throw salt onto the fire, so the fumes could put out the flames. If water was used to douse the fire, it would create a nasty mess in the grate.

In 1936, electricity was installed for lighting, and we also had two power points, one downstairs and one upstairs. Prior to this, gas was our means of lighting. We had a fitting in each room, controlled by two chains, one either side of the gas mantle. You pulled one for on, and the other for off. Light was produced via the mantle, which was made of very fine perforated asbestos; these were very fragile and had to be handled with great care. If you came home after dark, you needed to light a match to find your way across the room and then hopefully wouldn't poke the match through the mantle as you lit it.

To save money, only the rooms most used were lit up, the living room and kitchen; and the landing only when it was time for bed. Gas was supplied through 'penny in slot' meters that were set up to supply a little less than you paid for. When the meter was emptied, there was always a surplus to be returned to the consumer and this was regarded as Mum's pin money.

The fog that resulted from the use of coal fires and gas lighting was extremely dense; I have known visibility to be down to four or five feet. With only gas lamps in the street every eighty yards or so, people very easily lost their way and traffic came to a standstill. Worst of all was the grit that came from the fires that caused a lot of lung illnesses, especially in the elderly and in some of the worse fogs, hundreds of people died. These fogs came to be known as Smog.

Kitchens, often called sculleries, were sparse in facilities, a butler sink, a coal burning copper and a larder with a stone shelf to store butter, milk and meat, to keep cool. A shelf, high up on the wall was for keeping pots and pans and a stone floor ensured that the kitchen was rarely warm! Eventually we had a geyser fitted above the sink and this gave us hot water for washing and washing up, which saved us from having to boil water on the gas stove every time it was needed.

As there were no refrigerators, fresh food could not be kept long and had to be eaten before it went bad. Margarine was hard in Winter and melting in Summer. Not many working class families could afford butter.

Washing day was Monday. Dad used to light the fire under the boiler before he left for work so the water would be hot in time for Mum to start. Whites (sheets, towels and shirts etc.) were boiled first, and then put into the sink. Then Mum used a bar of Sunlight soap and a scrubbing board to give them a thorough scrubbing before rinsing; with a 'blue bag' in the last rinse to make the clothes whiter. Then they were put through the mangle. The mangle was turned by hand as the clothes were fed through the rollers and sometimes, if your fingers strayed too near the rollers, you could get some nasty bruises. After the mangle, the clothes were hung on to the line outside for drying. On wet days, they were hung anywhere in the house that could be found and for the rest of the day there was a very damp atmosphere in the house. Tuesday was ironing day. Two irons were needed for whilst one was in use the other was being heated on the gas stove. There were very few man-made fibres then, mostly clothes were made of cotton or wool. All the cottons had to be ironed including the sheets. I can remember Mum holding the irons to her face to test the temperature; too hot would leave iron shaped scorch marks and too cold would not remove the creases.

Sometimes, if the boiler was not watched closely, water would boil over and flood the kitchen and it was often not noticed until it reached the hallway. It took quite some time to clean up with only floor cloths, whilst down on hands and knees.

Friday night was bath night with water heated in the boiler in the kitchen and pumped by hand to the bath. As there was six in the family, bathwater was shared by us children, two at a time. By the time more water was heated for the later baths, it was ten o'clock before Mum's turn arrived. Sometimes, when the wind was in the wrong direction or if it was wet outside, the fire under the boiler was hard to light, resulting in a lot of bad temper, especially on Monday mornings as on these days washing didn't get finished until four or five o'clock in the afternoon.

School was organised differently to today: Infants 5-7 years, juniors 7-11 and seniors 11-14 and all did the same hours 9am-12noon, 1-45pm to 4pm. There was no homework, and not so many subjects and each day started with religious instruction. Class sizes were about 40 and were mixed sexes for the infants, but separated from then on. During the war, teachers were called up or away with the evacuees so classes often had over 50 pupils.

Free dinners were available for schoolchildren from poorer families, usually served in church halls and The Relief Office issued tickets for these. They also issued tickets for food, coal etc. which had to be used at specified dealers. No money was given. This was very shameful, but necessary when the father of the family was ill or out of work. The Relief Officers also used to visit the house to see if there was anything that could be sold to raise money, to save them paying out. Luckily this wasn't needed in ours.

There being no supermarkets then - small shops were plentiful for everyday items and two or three of each trade were in each parade of shops, making for local competition. All except the tobacconists closed at 5-30 pm each day, all day Sunday, and one half day during the week. You had to be a bit 'pushy' while shopping, as queuing was unknown until the war.

After the necessities were paid for, there was very little left for any luxuries like ice-cream etc... Our holidays usually consisted of a day at Southend, travelling there on a real steam train. Also, we sometimes had a Sunday out, going with Dad's cricket team to some pretty country place, although I hardly saw much more than the ground where the match was being played.

Working hours were long! In 1943, when I was 15 years old, my first job entailed working more than 47 hours a week, with one week holiday a year, plus fewer Bank Holidays and only TWO days at Christmas.

Evenings, with no television, were the time when we made our own entertainment, passing the time until we went to bed, with board games, jig saws, and model making. We had a wireless set, slightly misnamed, as it had to have a forty foot aerial and an earth wire before it could work. It also needed a battery about seven inches square, plus a smaller battery, known as a grid bias, and an acid accumulator, which had to be taken to the electrical shop be recharged every week, for 'tuppence'.

There were Saturday morning picture shows for kids at the local Methodist Church which was as large as many modern theatres, and for a penny you could see Flash Gordon, (science fiction), The Clutching Hand (murder and mystery) and a couple of cartoons. For this, you queued an hour, with a lot of pushing and shoving with a few fights taking place.

A visit to the Doctor cost two or three shillings, plus a further shilling or two for any medicine needed, dispensed next to the Surgery. There did not seem to be many tablets then, mostly medicines, so things bought from the chemists were usually tried first. Quinine, the most foul-tasting liquid ever conceived, was used if anyone had a temperature, the cure often being worse than the complaint. Iodine was used to treat cuts and grazes and it left a yellow stain on the skin that made the wound look twice the size it really was. It too, like quinine, was a painful cure, it really stung when put onto an open cut, but it was very good as an antiseptic.

There are a great number of things that have disappeared forever that evoke fond memories. From our bedroom window, I remember being able to see Gloster Gladiator bi-planes taking off from Hornchurch Aerodrome, but now there are at least two housing estates and a very large factory in between, instead of the country views we enjoyed before.

People were much friendlier then, lending cups of sugar etc. to each other, to see them through to end of the week, and child minding when needed, without expecting anything in return. Many families left their front door keys on a piece of string behind the letter box, so their children could get in without disturbing their mothers, or when their parents were out. Would you like to try that now?

Families were closer too; with no television to dominate the home, people were much more interested in each other's hobbies, offering advice in some cases. Also, most shared their mealtimes, adding to the togetherness that made you feel part of a whole unit

After school, kids could play in the street without the fear of traffic; no cars were parked in the streets, as only doctors or shop keepers seemed to own cars in my area. Many were the games that we played, most without any 'man made' equipment, only sticks and tin cans, sometimes someone provided a ball, and this doubled our number of games.

At the corners of most streets, there were shrubberies that came into use for hide and seek games - these areas have now been grassed over.

Opposite my house was an untended field and when the grass was long it was perfect for playing 'cowboys and Indians'. Years later, a local dairy 'Flints', brought their horses down to the field in the evening, the men riding bare back at full gallop which had everyone scattering for cover. Around 1945/6 these same dairymen came in the early evening selling fresh made ice cream straight from the churn. You had to take your own basin or jug out to them to be filled for just a few pence. I remember this was the first ice cream sold since 1940.

Most deliveries were made by horse drawn carts and the size of the Shire horses that pulled the coal cart was quite frightening for us so we used to keep a healthy distance from them. The baker had a high-sided barrow with two shafts that he used to pull it along.

Outside every school gate, home-made barrows, about the size of a large wardrobe, held all the sweets you could dream of, and sold from a farthing to a penny each. These barrows again had two shafts, for 'manhandling'. Rag and bone men came round during the day, offering money, china or toys for 'any old rags for china' was their cry. Knife grinders, umbrella repair men, boys selling shrimps and winkles on Sundays all helped to make the streets more exciting with their variety of calls.

One man had a small roundabout on the back of a cart that could carry two children at a time. He charged one empty jam-jar each and then had to push the roundabout by hand. Men from Dickie Birds and Eldorado's ice cream firms, used tricycles to carry their stock and were fairly regular salesmen coming round in the Summer, ringing their bells to let you know they were about - instead of the 'canned music' that you get now. If they arrived in the same street at the same time, strong words were often exchanged.

One memory that is very strong is of coming home from school on a Winter's day, and being given a slice of bread to toast on the open fire. With it was a nice dish of dripping (left over from the Sunday roast) with plenty of 'brown' on the bottom to spread on it.

Sometimes in the evenings, accompanied by Mum's piano playing, we would make up our own 'music' with a comb and paper, elastic bands around a matchbox, and a penny whistle, if we could find one.

The Becontree Estate in the thirties was very much neater and tidier, with all the front doors painted green, and evergreen hedges in front of all the houses. A gang of men using hand shears trimmed these hedges twice a year.

Today, with half the houses in private hands and all their 'home designed' additions and colours, with one or two cars parked on what used to be a front garden, the estate looks very untidy. Not too many years ago, you received a letter from the Council if your front garden was not kept in good order -progress? Nowadays, every side road is choked with cars parked wherever, it seems, the owners want, and cyclists have to ride on the pavements, as it is unsafe for them to use the road.

Supermarkets, built to supply cheap food and all in one shopping area, have killed off most of the small shops, leaving once thriving areas looking like ghost towns of the wild west, or else they have been taken over by banks, building societies, estate agents and various nationality takeaway ready cooked meals outlets.

A shop on the Heathway sold live eels from a box at the front of his display, and when as often happened, one or two escaped over the side, there was a general scattering of his women customers. Another sold faggots (a bit like meat-balls) or saveloys and pease pudding, on Saturday evenings. All hot, but you had to take your own large basin to carry them home in.

What shops that are left have metal shutters pulled down when closed, preventing vandals doing damage to the windows, so it is impossible now to go 'window shopping' as it was in the past. Then old people could walk in the streets at any time of the day without the fear of being mugged or harassed, and children played in the parks and streets in almost complete safety.

In days of old, when nights were cold,
And Winters were so bleak.
Chilblains as common as a cold,
Our firesides we'd seek.

Guessing games around the hearth,
The family all together,
The warmth engendered by our love,
Made us forget the weather

'Twas only a cat that slept on my bed,
But really wanted to sleep on my head

'Twas only a cat that woke me from sleep,
Two minutes before the alarm clock did bleep

'Twas only a cat that sat on my lap
& purred when I tickled her ears.

'Twas only a cat that lay on her back,
& waited to be brushed with the vac.

'Twas only a cat that followed me round
& watched whatever I did.

'Twas only a cat that jumped to the floor
& came to meet me behind the front door.

"Twas only a cat - That was Susie

I'm tired said the moon, I've been shining all night,
Not one cloud has come by to give me respite.

Be quiet growled the sun, I'm in need of a cure
I've been working all day with a high temperature

Alas, said the star, no one else has an inkling,
Of the work that I do, to keep myself twinkling.

Ah well, said the moon, I see no one is shirking so
I'll have to keep beaming and gleaming and working.

I've visited cathedrals, churches, castles too,
Lost count of country houses
that I have been to view.

Eaten clotted cream in Devon and tarts in Bakewell town.
Tasted Lardy cakes in Yorkshire
Barra Brith, of Welsh renown.

Been down slate mines in Snowdonia,
Climbed towers down in Kent
Splashed my feet all-round the coast,
"Swimming's not my bent".

From the leafy lanes of Dorset
To the wilds of Bodmin Moor,
From the hills and lakes of Cumbria
To the mud of Southend's shore.

I've travelled many Motorways
And tracks throughout the land,
And come to the conclusion
That this old country's GRAND.

I stopped to see the twinkle in her eye,
I only meant to glimpse it, passing by
But I found myself a' staring,
Very soon I was a' caring
For that saucy little twinkle in her eye

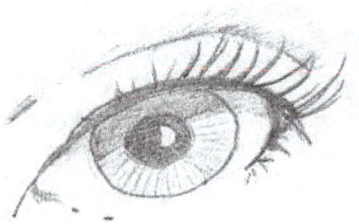

We got married one fine day in mid July
The church was filled with young men stopping by
But when I calmly said "I do"
She said the same to you
With that saucy little twinkle in her eye.

We settled down and got ourselves a flat
And there's nothing much remarkable in that
'Til one day she said "just maybe,
I'm expecting our first baby
But for now, it's just a twinkle in your eye".

FOOLS GOLD

My, it's cold! I never knew it could be this cold. I'm sitting in the heated carriage of a train in the middle of nowhere and if I look out of the window it's snow, snow, and in the distance more snow. With my two friends Josh and Walter I'm on the way to the town of Arnuk at the end of the line. The temperature outside is 15 below and I'm frightened to think what it will be like further north.

We are now in Alaska, after travelling wearily across the width of Canada. It has only been a few weeks since we started, but it seems much longer. This is supposed to be the season when the weather begins to warm up, but even the people that we have met on our journey are wondering if it will ever happen.

Chance started us on this painful trip, when Josh, who was an auctioneer's assistant specialising in house clearances, found an old book covered in dust and beginning to fall apart, at the bottom of a wardrobe. A sheet of notepaper, very brittle, was protruding from inside the back cover of the book and Josh carefully removed it. On it, in very clear handwriting, was the bald statement that the writer was going to join the army and fight for England, but when he returned he would go and retrieve the gold that his father had hidden. The letter was dated June 1915.

A second part gave precise instructions of how to get to where his father had left the gold that came from his plot during the great gold rush. The father had been killed in a barroom fight soon after sending his young wife and son home to England but it had been his intention to follow as soon as he had cashed his cache, so to speak. The son never made it home from Flanders.

That's why the three of us are sitting here, being shaken about, thoroughly bored with the monotony of the view, freezing cold and hungry with our next meal not due for another three hours. We all said we came for adventure but greed was our secret motive, if we did but admit it.

Arnuk at last! Rising stiffly from our seats we gathered together our luggage and stepped down from the train and it would be a gross understatement to say we were surprised by what we saw. Whenever I re-live that moment, shock and horror, are words that still spring to mind! Arnuk was but fifty or sixty wooden buildings, with high sloping roofs and very small windows, and only a couple with more than one storey but at least finding our 'hotel' was easy enough, it was opposite the station with the word 'hotel' in letters three feet high on the roof.

We stayed a few days, catching up on some sleep and hired a guide with dog teams, to take us to where we hoped to find the gold.

We left at dawn and it was snowing, but we hoped to cover about twenty miles, half way to our destination. Every time we stopped the guide complained about the size of his fee, which had been agreed before starting out and the second day was a repeat of the first, except that the weather had improved.

Making camp that night we were in an excited mood, knowing we were close to our goal, but after two exhausting days on the trial, we slept heavily expecting our guide to wake us with a hot drink, as on the previous morning. When we finally crept from the tent there was no guide, no dogs, only the smaller of the two sledges. Some of the food was missing too but thinking he might have gone to get wood to eke out our supply of oil, we did not worry overmuch.

We got the map out, looking around for the landmarks on it and could recognise two hills. We took a bearing from them and walked nearly a mile until we came to a partially frozen lake. We couldn't find the rock arches that were supposed to be in a valley close by and puzzling over this, we made our way back to camp.

Arriving back we found our guide had not returned, so rushed to prepare a meal before it got dark. Walter complained about his feet hurting, and we found that two of his toes were frostbitten. In the morning with still no sign of our guide we discovered that some of our clothes, food and a large chunk of our money were missing, so then we knew he wasn't coming back!

Left with only one sledge to take the luggage and no dogs to pull it, Walter's bad foot, and being virtually lost in a wilderness, we knew we were in big trouble. Knowing we would not be able to walk back the way we had come, even if we could remember the route and the weather closing in again, we decided to make our way to what looked like a small forest which had been noticed by Josh whilst we out yesterday. We thought it would give us more shelter and provide wood to light a fire.

We packed only the most essential gear and walked, but within a very short distance the pain in Walter's foot became too much for him to carry on, so we put him onto the sledge which left Josh and I to carry the gear and pull him as well.

It was easier to travel on the lake for most of the distance and we trudged for hours, utterly exhausted until finally we reached the forest as the daylight was fading. Managing only to pitch the tent, we crept into our sleeping bags, sleeping almost as our heads touched the piles of clothes we used as pillows.

Josh and I awoke after just an hour or so, very cold and hungry, we realised that we had not eaten for many hours. Close to our camp was a fallen tree, and we set about collecting wood and lighting a fire. Soon, a good blaze was going, and just as important, we had a hot drink and food inside us. Survival by the minute was all that we could think of, all hope was gradually draining from us. We returned to the tent to sleep for the rest of the night and nobody noticed that the fire was flaring up close to the fallen tree. The flames reached it and the whole tree caught alight but in the tent, helped by the extra heat, we were so fast asleep we did not notice it.

Hours later, actually many hours, I thought I heard voices and reasoned it was the next stage of our mental and physical condition, in downward slide. In this dream-like state, I felt my shoulder shaken and heard a voice saying, "Can you hear me? ". It was repeated twice again before I realised it was real and responding to the call I stirred and turned over, found a man almost buried in fur clothes, tapping gently on my face and telling me to wake up and that I was safe now. I remember being put on a stretcher, placed in a large vehicle with caterpillar tracks and being given a hot drink, which seemed to have a taste of brandy. As the truck bounced alongside the lake, the next two hours were a blur.

I awoke in a white room and had tubes sticking out of me from places I don't like to mention and Josh and Walter were in beds close to mine. Walter had a very large dressing on his foot, which was suspended from a contraption of pulleys and a middle-aged nurse was sitting reading a magazine at the other side of the room.

Wondering where we were, but not really worried as after the last two weeks here was so much more comfortable, I gazed around the room until the nurse noticed my movements. She came over to me and started to check my condition without answering any of my questions, (later I found she was Russian). She left the room and a doctor came soon after, doing his own checks and asking how we had come to be in such a dangerous situation. After hearing a little of my tale, he explained that the smoke from the burning tree had alerted some of the workers who came to find out what would cause a fire in such a remote area.

He told me we were at a hydroelectric station, built at the lower end of the lake, which was really a reservoir, and we were in the sickbay where the halftracks had brought us. He prescribed rest, warmth and good food and we had no argument with that.

Feeling much better the next day, I told him of the treachery of our guide, and immediately he radioed the authorities in Arnuk and reported what we had told him. I asked if he knew of the three arches across the river, supposedly near where our first camp had been, and he said that he would ask around. Josh's recovery caught up with my own and soon we were allowed out of bed to wander around the rest of the complex. It was amazing that in the middle of such a wilderness this huge place had been built. The dam itself was over two hundred feet high and four hundred feet across, and the power that it created was carried on pylons for more than eighty miles to the south and supplied thousands of homes.

A worker who was about sixty years old remembered the three arches, but said they had to be blown up fifteen years ago, as they might have been a hazard if left under water level. He said it was a good thing they were or they would never have found the gold that was uncovered by the blast and shared the reward for it. We asked what had happened to the gold and he said 'the find' was advertised in newspapers but nobody claimed it. It had been used to build a children's hospital in the city and we were astonished to hear that it was worth nearly half a million dollars - a lot of money in anyone's language and I think our expressions told the story.

After, we confessed that it was the gold that had brought us here and we spent the next few days and weeks wondering and thinking of what might have been.

We heard that our guide had been arrested in Arnuk as he tried to sell some of our clothes and equipment and was now awaiting trial. That would probably be three months away and we didn't want to wait around that long, as money was getting a problem. We were still a long way from home, so with our heartfelt thanks to our rescuers, and a reluctant farewell to all those who had looked after us, we were taken by helicopter, with Walter strapped on a stretcher, to Canada.

Arriving in the afternoon, we first went with Walter to the local hospital and he was admitted to have two toes removed. Josh and I found a telegraph office and wired home for more money then had a meal and found a hotel for a couple of nights whilst we waited for our cash to arrive.

Two days on a train, a four-hour flight, finally brought us to where we could get a trans-Atlantic flight home. It seemed a never ending journey but eventually Heathrow came and went and Josh and I were on a train to the west, thinking of that other train journey when we were so cold, but hopeful.

After a few days rest, I decided it was time to get dressed up and see the lads at the pub to tell my tale of woe. At least it should be good for a few free drinks, As I put on my jacket, I checked the pockets and found a lottery ticket, bought before going away. Throwing it onto the table, my young brother grabbed it saying it was probably worth a fortune, and he would look it up on the Internet whilst I was out.

After a great night out, I arrived home late and found him waiting up with the grand news that I had won a 'tenner' - almost! Unfortunately the ticket was three weeks out of date.

...he managed to dodge my attempts to kill him.

Man's greed is as old as man himself,
That's what we were told, when at school.
But when gold was found beneath the ground,
Man's greed for this gold, increased a hundredfold
And created a thousand fools.

JACOB'S WILL

It all started with old Jacob, way back in the 1870's and actually it wasn't all his fault, more the fault of his two sons Samuel and Charles. They were twins, born ten minutes apart to Adelaide, Jacob's second wife. His first wife succumbing to typhoid fever ten years before, he'd waited a long time to get a son and heir, and was doubly joyful when, at last the twins were born. But he paid dearly a few weeks later, for Adelaide died from birth complications.

Jacobs's sister Emmie moved in to take care of the boys, and she being childless made them her purpose in life but Jacob took very little interest in them. He threw his whole energies into running the farm, which had been in his family's care for many generations, building it up so there would be enough to pass on to each son when the time came when he couldn't manage it himself.

He never accepted that Samuel was the eldest, saying it was only the fact they could not come out at the same time which made any the difference. He was meticulous in the way he shared everything equally concerning the farm and sometimes took on extra jobs himself, to make thing fair. Even trips to the village to take produce to their shop, was done alternately.

As the boys grew up, different temperaments began to show and Samuel took on the cattle side of the farm, and Charles the sheep. Luckily the farm had grown big enough to include both kinds of habitat, for it wrapped itself around the village of Newton Green, and had well-watered pastureland to the east, and rolling hills to the north and west.

Old Jacob finally met his maker at the grand old age of 93, but not before making his will which he hoped would end the bickering between his two sons, once and for all. Another shop was to be purchased in the village, to stop any arguments on that score and Samuel was to have all the land to the east and Charles, the land to the north and west. The farmhouse had been already been split into two some years before, to keep the brothers apart, which seemed to satisfy them both at the start, as it meant that they did not have to see each other very often. Even the funeral arrangements had been made by old Jacob so there was not much trouble when papers had to be signed.

Jacob was laid to rest on a Thursday but on Friday the troubles began!

Samuel had always being very disgruntled at not being regarded the eldest and Charles' resentment at Samuel's attitude had begun so early in their lives neither could remember just when it did start. Now it progressed rapidly, as each was as pig-headed as the other and 'fur flew' very often. As they grew up, physical violence had gradually given way as both realized that it could be very painful, but sniping and silly tricks took over.

One time, part of the fence between the farms was blown down in a gale and Charles and some of his men quickly went out during the gale, to patch it up. They found that part of the fence at an odd shaped piece of land, was beyond repair so Charles joined the fence onto a small part of Samuel's land to make it secure. His intention was to make it good later.

Although this area of the land was only twenty or thirty square yards, Samuel threatened to take legal action and that got Charles' back up. Solicitors' letters flew back and forth until the local vicar intervened and brought them to their senses. They then shared the costs and put the fence right.

Charles managed to buy a shop, almost opposite his brother's in the village and just a short distance from his own pub. Fortunately, there were two pubs in the village, so each brother had his favourite and declared he wouldn't be seen dead in the other one!

Jacob's wake was held in both pubs but many of the mourners went home early, afraid to show any favouritism to either. The rest shared their time in each pub, but that still did not please Samuel or Charles.

Aunt 'Emmie' who had raised them, was not any help. She insisted on calling them Sammy and Charlie but Samuel refused to answer to Sammy, as he thought it sounded common. Charles on the other hand, rather liked being called Charlie as it made him feel like 'one of the boys' yet he would not be outdone by his brother -so stuck to his proper name as well.

Emmie was rapidly going senile and often miss-recalled anecdotes from the past which kept the pot boiling, such as the time she remembered Sammy was born ten days before Charles.

Eventually, Samuel's son took over the dairy farm and a few years later Charles' daughter Hannah, inherited the sheep. If anybody in the village thought that a woman taking over one of the farms would soften the feud, they had not met Hannah. "Hard hearted Hannah" as she became known but only when she was not in hearing distance.

Selling her wool harvest further away, she got a much higher price and used the money to cut most of the prices in her shop. But Samuel's son David was not as good a businessman as his father and could not compete with this latest attack. He resorted to rougher tactics, and as a result, one morning before reaching the village the cart delivering milk from an outside dairy to Hannah's shop had one of the wheels mysteriously fall off and was not able to arrive until the afternoon. Another time, a tree that could only have been put there by tractor, was found lying across the road, exactly where it made a long detour necessary.

Year after year, so it went on, even when David's son, Robert took over the dairy. Hannah had surprised everyone in the village by getting married as nobody thought there was a man strong enough or foolish enough to take her on. Sadly, although married life began to soften her attitude it wasn't to last long for she slipped off the top of a ladder whilst cleaning the gutters on the shearing shed, hit her knee on a log that was lying around and gangrene set in. Surgeons left it long to amputate and she died in a few months. Her husband, Arthur only survived her by eight months and left the farm to his only daughter, Sally who was Hannah's stepdaughter.

Sally knew nothing about sheep and employed a manager to run the farm whilst she concentrated on the shop. In the beginning, both shops had been named Bilsom's which had always confused the villagers. Now she re-named hers 'Sally's' and expanded it to contain a Post Office and also sold a greater variety of goods. This created extra trade and eroded Robert's profits so that his shop only just paid it's way and not able to expand or cut his prices, he took to almost petty reprisals.

Sally started to write on her shop window in whitewash, special offers or items that she wanted to 'push' so during the night, Robert took to rubbing out some of the letters and altering the whole meaning of what Sally had meant. FRESH BREAD DAILY became F I SH B AD DAILY and so on.

Sally ignored all this and finding she had a bit of spare time in the evenings started a Guide and Brownie group in the church hall, and before the sheep were let onto her land, she organised camps for the girls.

Robert wouldn't be outdone, so he organised a Scout Group, but was disturbed to find that he had to attend some of the same training evenings as Sally. He managed to keep to other side of the hall but many were the glances that flashed from side to side.

Fund raising to repair the spire, the vicar suggested a village fete and as the church was a particularly important one in the area, all the villagers, and many from the neighbouring villages wanted to take part. Many committees were formed to organise the various activities and Sally and Robert, involved with Scouts and Guides were co-opted onto a few.

One evening a few days before the BIG DAY, Sally was busy rehearsing her Guides in a play showing the history of the village whilst Robert was fixing bunting and lights across the street. He was just coming down his ladder when it slipped on the cobbled road and he fell heavily onto the pavement. He lay without moving and his helper running to his side, found he was not breathing. Knowing that Sally was a First-Aider and that she was in the church hall nearby he shouted out for her. Sally came out and quickly summed up the situation and started to give Robert artificial respiration where he lay. After only a few 'blows' Robert responded and as Sally started to raise her head to take another breath, he whispered to her, " I've wanted a kiss with you for a long time", " So have I " she replied and gave him a kiss that took his breath right away

- Jacob R.I.P.

DÉJÀ VU

I had often heard people talking about the feeling of déjà vu they had experienced, when entering a strange house of building for the first time. I pooh poohed their talking as over imagination or some such, especially I they had spend a whole holiday there, and had time to get used to the place. That was until this happened to me…

I had booked into an isolated cottage in Dorset, but it was so isolated I had trouble finding it, but I finally arrived, tired and grumpy, too tired even to notice the giant hollyhocks by the front door.

After hauling my bags along the path to the front door, then grovelling under the doormat for the very large key, I finally managed to open the door. As it swung back with much squealing and groaning, I looked straight into the living room; and then the thought came into the back of my mind "I know this place". Frowning, as I stepped in, I looked around and felt the warmth that many people had spoken about. Fetching my bags in and closing the door, my next thought was "A nice cup of tea, and then to bed".

I think it is about time I introduce myself; my name is Peter, and I am an artist, specialising in boats, harbours, and costal thins and the like. I'm no good at figures or anything too modern. I spend a few weeks every year going around the coast of Britain sketching with pencil or pastels any views I fancy, until I have forty or fifty to take back to my studio in Brentwood in Essex, to use (or not) in my paintings.

Going into the kitchen, the first thing I saw was a tray with most of the 'makings' that I was looking for, but when I turned the mug around to reach the handle, I saw that it had my initials on it, in large letters. Trying to ignore this, I realised I needed a spoon and started to move my hand towards the nearest drawer, but it seemed to hesitate of its own accord and move on to the next one where I withdrew the spoon I wanted… How?? Why?? "The sooner I've finished the tea, the sooner I can get up to bed, and snuggle down under that nice blue duvet… "This is getting silly…"

To take my mind off the strange things that were happening, I decided to think about the painting that was waiting in my studio; what colour should I do the small cabin cruiser in the foreground …and maybe paint out the red sails in the distance? These, and similar thoughts filled the time it took to drink up my tea and lock the doors. Picking up my bags, I carried them upstairs to the first room I came to and quickly got myself ready for bed. Soon I starting slipping under the THICK BLUE DUVET - oh no, not again! I surrendered to it all and to my surprise as soon as I lay down I fell into a beautiful, peaceful sleep.

In the morning, thoroughly refreshed I hurriedly emptied the rest of my bag and organised my sketching and drawing materials; sorting out what I needed to take with me for the day. Eventually I was ready to start but then found that the front door had jammed and it took a lot of heaving to haul it open. At last in the car, I set the 'satnav' for Lulworth Cove and the real adventure.

When I arrived, I stood and stared for a while, but decided not to do much drawing there as most people would know the place and I wanted to keep my work personal to me. Around the corner at Durdle Door it was a different matter; with the rocks twisted in so many ways I spend quite some time there. On my way home ('Did I say home? I meant the cottage') I took a diversion to Abbotsbury - I didn't know there were so many swans in England!

Next day, Weymouth with its wide sweeping bay had much to interest me and I spent many hours there. The size of Portland Harbour surprised me and Chesil Beach has to be seen to be believed.

And so the days went by, including a day off from the seaside, looking at the different thatch at Burton Bradstock and enjoying a ploughman's lunch at one of the local pubs.

The Satnav didn't have any protection from my fumbling the next morning, so I got completely lost but thought I found the coast when I got to Bridport. I then found it was still a good way away but when West Bay finally came into sight, it made up for all the hassle.

It was just the place I had been looking for, seemed to have everything I needed and soon I settled down to my work. I noticed a huge bank of cloud building up in the west, but was only interested in how to incorporate it into my drawings. When it started raining it as an immediate deluge so that by the time I had protected my work I was drenched and though I virtually ran back to my car water was coming out of my shoes. But the Satnav didn't let me down on the way home... 'I'm doing it again!' I thought!

The door opened easily at the first push and the water seemed to heat faster than before so it was not long before I was soaking my cares away in a hot bath.

The next day, I spent all at West Bay and when I finished, I had enough drawings and pastels to last me a lifetime.

The morning soon came when it was time to go back to Brentwood. The sun shone as I arose but began to cloud over as I pulled my bags out from under the bed. The door jammed a little as I took the first bag out but on returning inside, I found the second bag had some of its contents which I knew I had packed carefully, strewn around. I repacked, took a last look around, making for the door I had left open and found it shut and stuck fast... It took more than two minutes to free it and I sighed with relief when I closed the door behind me, putting the key back where I had found it.

It was a few days after I had got home to my flat and studio that was above the antique shop managed by my girlfriend, before we started to inspect the sketches I'd brought back.

Our method was for her to pick one at a time, take a good look then pass it to me with her comments - good or bad but always honest.

We had gone through most of them before, as she lifted the next one her eyes and mouth seemed to open wide, before she stared at the drawing saying 'You told me you couldn't draw cottages and people, but this is perfect!' As she passed it to me she said, 'The features are so good they almost look like u....' then she stopped. I peered at the sketch for many minutes - there was THE cottage with the red hollyhocks in the garden but in the doorway stood two people - the man on the right a slightly older image of me, and the lady... yes, you've guessed it....

Are you still searching for the end of that rainbow?
The one with such a huge crock of gold,
And are people still saying, it's time to stop dreaming
If so, just tell them this is what I have been told,

That a man needs a dream to cling onto,
Something to aim for in life
A dream that will last him forever,
In this world full of trouble and strife.

Don't give up, carry on with your dreaming
Though it may not come true,
A dream made by you
Can still be as strong as a friend,
Follow it through to the end,

T'was the night before Christmas

The Museum was shut.
The house wasn't empty. Anything but.
Agnes de Valence was rushing around.
Old Bonham, her lover,
She just could not discover.

She searched all the cupboards,
And behind every chair,
But old Mr. Bonham was clearly not there.

She walked through young Henshaw,
Who was writing a book,
He said when he had time, he'd help her to look.

When he heard all the fuss,
Sir Nicholas Coote,
Said if I had my way I'd give him the boot.

His snooty wife Eleanor,
Smiling quite smugly,
Said, I think that our Agnes is getting so ugly.

Eventually, poor Agnes
Found the old feller, (ouch)
He was counting his money, down in the cellar

Meanwhile, Thomas May
As he did every day,
Was making it clear, that he wasn't here

THE COTTAGE ON THE MOOR

The candle spluttered to stay alight, but lost the battle to the draught that came suddenly from the direction of the door. With only the glow from the dying embers of the fire to help me, I groped for the torch I had kept close so I could find my way around the inside of the cottage, for I only had candles for illumination at that time. I found it and pointing it at the door, saw straight away that the door was completely closed and the board was still in place.

Before I had time to wonder what caused the draught, there was a hissing noise behind me, as if water had been poured onto the fire, and the last faint glow disappeared and the smell of sulphur mixed with the smell of burning meat, assailed my nostrils...

I had rented the cottage in the middle of the Yorkshire Moors so that I could concentrate on writing a book, which until then had been going well.

The day had started badly, with the temperature well below what it had been in the last few weeks then rain arrived before lunch. I'd got soaked going out to the outhouse to start the generator, but it refused to start, even after I had tried for more than half an hour. Now this!

The room had turned icy cold and I turned the torch towards the fireplace, hoping to see what had happened to the fire, but before the light reached there, the torch was torn from my hand, flying with great force at the chimney breast, where it shattered into many pieces. I was left in total darkness.

In panic I turned to where I thought there was the door to the kitchen but only succeeded in falling over a chair and hitting my head on a corner of the table. Slightly dazed, I lay on the floor as a low moaning started and it gradually increased in volume until it reached a scream that filled my ears and brain, to the exclusion of everything else. Whether from fear or cold, I do not know, but drenched in sweat, I shook and reaching out, tried to orientate myself and make an escape through the kitchen door. My hand touched something colder even than the room and I felt along the object until, with revulsion, I made out the shape of a human hand... a man's hand, by it's size and the hair on the arm.

As my hand travelled back again, more horror for it ended a few inches above the elbow where the flesh felt crisp to touch around the protruding bone. I snatched my hand away fast, and luckily contacted the frame of the kitchen door, and as I reached for the handle, the screaming, rose to new heights. In one swift action, I pulled myself upright, turned the handle, dived through the door and slammed it after me. The screaming stopped.

Shaking like a leaf, I fumbled back to the drawer where the spare candles and matches were kept and using seven or so matches, I managed to get one to stay alight and lit all the candles I could find. No sound at all came now from the other room, but I wasn't going anywhere near it.

Finding my bottle of brandy, I poured a generous measure and downed it all in one gulp then as the warmth rapidly calmed me, I poured another and took it to the table in the middle of the room. Looking at my watch it was 10.15 pm and another seven or eight hours to daylight, which was a long time to fill. To ensure there were enough to last I doused some of the candles and sat pondering what could I do to pass the time until morning?

The rain seemed heavier even than before, so there was no point in going out and the nearest neighbour was over four miles away and as I sat listening to the ticking of the clock, the rain beating against the window, I saw a number of books on the top shelf of the dresser. Thinking to take my mind off what had happened in the next room, I looked through them and found the third was titled "Strange Tales of the Moors", written nearly ninety years ago.

As the title suggested, these were short stories and articles about accidents in the coalmines and disappearances and murders that were never solved, and the affect they had on people in the district. I had read nearly half the book when my attention was grabbed with something akin to shock.

I was reading a tale about an old couple living in an isolated cottage and how on a bitterly cold day, the wife had lit a very big fire, and had a very large pot of stew simmering on the side. Her seventy year old husband was out rescuing some of his lambs in awful weather and she was waiting his return.

When he arrived home he went to the fire to warm himself, but tripping on the edge of the rag mat, he hit his head on the mantelshelf and fell onto the fire. His wife was too frail to help him, so the unfortunate man burned until only his arm was left and she fell down beside him. As they both burnt, the bones of her fingers entwined with his.

Startled, I looked at the date of the event, and checked the calendar on the back of the door – it was one hundred years ago today, exactly!

A WHOLE STORY

If you've ever had the pleasure to wander over the Yorkshire Moors, you must remember the strange outcrop of rocks interspersed with mostly shallow dips and holes in the ground that occur in a few areas. I was looking at one of these places a couple of years ago, when my attention was drawn to a middle aged man who was searching in a very small area of holes, time and time again. After a while I gradually moved nearer to him, trying to see just at what he was looking.

Noticing my interest in his activities, he came over to me, and, after introducing himself, asked if I knew this area well, and if I did, did I know of any caves or lakes anywhere near.

After I admitted that I could not help him in that, I suggested, as the sun was beginning to dip further towards the skyline, we should adjourn to one of the pubs in the nearby village for dinner, and while there ask the locals if they could answer his question. This we did, as we waited for our meals to arrive, but no one knew of any caves, even the people who had lived there all their lives.

He was very quiet throughout the meal, but at the end offered drinks at the bar, when he would explain the cause of his search, and this is how his story unfolded...

' I suppose you think I'm a bit paranoid over this but when I explain Just what happened nearly twenty years ago, you will see why I wanted to try and dismiss the subject from my mind.

I was an archaeologist, and came to this area to explore, and try to explode the myths that were about; especially the one that the holes were dug by Prehistoric people.

I had been working for about an hour or so, when I thought I saw a strange inscription on a standing stone, something like a matchstick man with a very large head. Thinking it was probably only graffiti I went to get a closer look, but my foot slipped and I fell into the hole in front of the stone. Halfway down (I think) my head hit the stone side of the hole, and I blacked out.

I partially awoke when I felt water falling onto my lips, which was very welcome. As the pains in my head receded, I began to hear strange grunts and a slightly softer sound. Eventually I managed to open my eyes to see a face looming over mine, a face that was hardly recognizable as human. It was covered in hair, so much so that his beard tangled with the hair on his chest, eyes so deep set that they were almost impossible to see. The smell that came from him was so acrid it nearly choked me. He grunted again, and was answered by the sound of another voice, this one much softer, that I had heard before. Turning my head carefully, I could see the other person clearly, an obvious female, with no facial hair, gazing down at me.'

At this point I interrupted him, so I could replenish our glasses, and give him time to recover, as he was getting very agitated. Ten minutes went by before he carried on with his narrative...

'As I came more aware of my surroundings, I realised that we were in a cave with daylight coming in from a few yards away. On the middle of the floor at the opening I could see a fire burning. The woman rose from beside me and went towards the fire and came back with a large shell full of a brown liquid and pieces of meat. I suddenly realised that I was very hungry; the smell from pot was very inviting. I started looking for a spoon for the liquid, when the woman, with a version of sign language, indicated that I should use my fingers for the meat and just drink from the shell. The food was surprisingly good; I could feel the strength growing inside me.

Later, rising from my bed, which I found was a pile of dried grass; I walked slowly toward the front of the cave, wanting to find out just where I was. But all I could see was an area of long grass, and further away, a thin line of trees through which I could make out was the sea.

Disappointed, I made my way back to my pile of grass when the man, (who I named Ugha, for that was the sound he mostly used) made signs that I should go to sleep.

In the morning, even though it was nowhere near daylight, Ugha had gone, and 'Mum' (I called her that, for that was what she reminded me of) explained with her sign language and much laughter, that he had gone hunting, and, in a few days, we would all go together, as long I could learn to use a bow. I started to practice as soon as possible, but it took a long time before I could get near a target. If I had to rely on my own efforts I would be starving within days.

A few days later, before sunrise, we were off with Ugha leading at a very fast pace, and soon we were in much thicker woodland. Mum started to gather herbs and things, while I stood guard, or looked as if I was. Ugha came back with a couple of small animals tied to his belt. It was time to move again. Soon we were all trying to get to windward of a small group of deer, but concentrating on this, we did not hear the approach of a small group of men, until arrows came into us thick and fast, unfortunately one of the first arrows hit Mum in the neck and, she fell in a heap.

Seeing this, Ugha went berserk, lashing out with the bone club that had been hanging from his belt, I helped him as much as I could by throwing stones, and anything else I could find, until an arrow pierced my upper arm. As soon as the raiders had disappeared, Ugha went over to Mum's body, sat beside her and started to gently stroke her face, all the time low moaning sounds coming from his throat. After a while, he gently removed the arrow from her neck, picked her up and led at a fast pace back to the cave. I followed as fast as I could, not wanting to be lost in the woods. Ugha seemed to have forgotten me, or was blaming me for what happened, I didn't know.

Reaching the cave at last, Ugha made signs to me to help him dig a grave for Mum, but when I pointed to the arrow in my arm, he came over and studied it for a moment, then almost casually broke the shaft off near to the skin of my arm. The pain was excruciating for a while, but I helped Ugha as much as I could to lay her into the ground and cover her with heavy stones to stop the wolves from disturbing her.
Only when he was satisfied with our efforts did he turn to me. The arrowhead was nearly protruding from the other side of my arm, and he suddenly pushed the broken shaft further in until the head came through the skin, He grabbed at it and pulled. I passed out.'

It must have been a few minutes before I noticed he had stopped talking, so engrossed was I in his story, and glancing at him, could see that his mind had completely withdrawn from the surroundings. Not wishing to disturb him straightaway, I concentrated on my own reactions to his tale trying to evaluate it, coming to the natural conclusion that it was result of the blow to head. I gently spoke to him, and when he became aware of me, suggested we should both seek our beds and sleep on what he had told me.

I walked him back to where he was staying, as he did not seem safe to be on his own.
We met after lunch on the following day, and as the weather was fine decided to walk the moors again, to a place that would take his mind from his troubles, but after only a short time and much to my surprise he started once again on his tale...
'It was the rain that woke me, the rain that looked as if it was set in for the day. I rose and started to walk, the rain getting heavier as time passed, soaked me through, there seemed nowhere to shelter, only short prickly bushes sparsely spread among the grass. Well into the afternoon, as well as I could judge, a grey building emerged from the gloom ahead; it turned out to be a fort of some kind, built on an escarpment with the highest part facing north. As I approached the doorway, two men obviously guards, by the weapons they were wearing, appeared on the battlements above it, shouting down at me in a language I at first could not understand, but eventually realised it was a form of Latin that I knew.
They were demanding to know who I was, and what I wanted. When I stated the obvious, food and shelter, the door opened and two other men came through the door and escorted me in, holding me tightly and staring at my clothes. I stared back at theirs, leather skirts and brass breastplates reminding me of Roman soldiers. I was marched into the largest building in the enclosure, and there made to wait. Eventually I was led into the presence of a very stern faced giant of a man, obviously an officer, who stared down at me, I stared back at him, trying to feel brave, he came over to me and felt my coat, and was puzzled by my trousers.
All the time he was doing this, he kept asking the same questions again and again, getting more bad-tempered as time went on. Finally I was bundled by two of his minions down to

the cellars of the building and thrown into a cell which already contained more than twenty men, all of whom seemed to be sleeping or very lethargic.

In the morning, after being fed a thin gruel, we were taken out, led by two guards with whips, to an area some half a mile away, and made to pick up the largest boulders we could, and carry them back to the fort to strengthen the walls. It was very exhausting work, and at the end of the day, a little more food was given to us before we were led to our cell to sleep.

In the morning one of the men was dead, and two of us were told to take him to top of the north wall and throw him over, at this point there was a drop of over a hundred feet to the river below. This seemed their way of getting rid of slaves. The north wall extended east and west of the fort, as far as the eye could see, guards patrolled the wall, all looking north, as if afraid of attack.

Many days passed, I lost count of how many, escape looked impossible, and hope was fading, until one day the Governor brought round a group of richly dressed men and women on horseback, to show off his power. As the group neared where I stood, the stone I was holding slipped from my hands and rolled a little towards the horses, one of which skittered away and nearly unseated the lady rider. In an instant a whip snaked out and landed across my shoulders causing me to cry out in pain, hardly hearing the shouted orders of the Governor.

A burly guard picked me up, ran with me wriggling in his arms, into the fort and up to the north wall. Realising what was going to happen to me, I grabbed at anything I could, but his strength was too much for me and he wrenched my hands away and threw me over the wall and I was falling...'

At this point he stopped talking, started staggering and waving his arms like windmills, I had to catch him before he fell, and lowered him to the ground, talking softly all the while until he calmed down, eventually sinking into a deep sleep which lasted for more than an hour. All the while, I was thinking that this was a man who needed serious help, much more than I could offer. When he awoke, he wanted to carry on with the walk, but I led him around in a circle and back to the village.

On arrival, he made straight for the bar, ordered a brandy, and downed it in one swallow, said he was tired and went up to his room. I didn't see him for the rest of the evening, I spoke to the landlord, and asked him to keep an eye on for him, and this he agreed to do.
Managing to get an appointment with a local G.P. early the following morning, I explained the situation to him as much as possible. He replied that it was very puzzling, and only a psychologist could really answer the problem, but his only advice was to keep him away from the subject if I could, until he returned home.

There was no chance of that, however, for when I got back to my room, he was there knocking on the door. Forcing himself to be calm, he said he wanted to finish his story today. I tried to talk him out of it, saying it was putting too much strain on him but he was very insistent, so I led him to one of the seats on the village green. The small parcel he carried, he carefully laid on the seat on the other side, so that I could not see it. We were hardly settled before he started...

'I felt water (I thought) cascading onto my head, running down my clothes to my feet and beyond, the sudden shock brought me to a standstill wondering where it came from, I looked up just in time to see a chamber pot being withdrawn into a casement window, which closed at once. The smell coming from my clothes and hair, almost made me vomit.

I looked around, trying to make sense of my surrounding; I was in a very narrow street, the tops of the buildings nearly touching, cutting out the sunlight. Walking faster to find some space, I moved to the side but, just as I got there, heard shouting ahead, and soon a young boy came running towards me, followed by a mob of about twenty men and women, all shouting " Stop Thief ". As the boy passed me, I felt something thrust into my hand; soon he disappeared round the next corner.

When the mob had gone, I found a quiet spot where I wasn't overlooked, I glanced at what the boy had put in my hand. I was a brown leather drawstring purse. Opening it carefully I saw it contained a number of what I took to be coins, very old coins. I hid the purse in my pocket, and walked on, thoroughly bewildered by my surroundings, not knowing where I was, or where to go, I didn't see or hear the horse coming towards me. The last thing I felt was one of the horse's hooves hitting the side of my head.

That's nearly it, let me rest for a while, and I promise I will finish.'

He looked more peaceful now than I had ever seen him, and leaving him to relax. I was quietly relieved that his story was nearly over. I just sat by him, waiting when he "came to" with a start, saying...

'Sorry I kept you, but now will come to the point... I felt water trickling onto my lips, and a cool cloth bathing my forehead, and started to open my eyes, but the light was too bright and I closed them again. Whoever was treating me must have realised this and dimmed it, and I tried again. This time I could see a nurse, in a dark blue uniform looking at me, but talking into a telephone. When she came back to me, she started talking softly, saying she was glad to see me, as I had been asleep for more than a week.

Doctors came, then more, all asking questions until I fell asleep.

My wife came, smiling and crying at the same time, my son came, looking worried.

At last, after a week, I was told I could go home. My clothes were brought to me. I had to wait until they "rescued" the contents of my pockets from the safe. Apart from the normal things from them, like money, keys etc., I was given these'.

As he said the last few words, he handed me the packet he had brought with him, and I tipped the contents out carefully on to the seat between us. A stained arrowhead with three inches of splintered shaft, a brassy looking badge of some kind, and last, but not least, a brown drawstring purse that rattled as it hit the seat...

We talked for a very long time, not just about his story, but many other things, until rain interrupted us, so we retired to a nearby bar and drunk the rest of the night away. In the morning he had gone, leaving only a note, thanking me for my help, which I could not remember giving, and wishing me luck. That was the last I ever heard of him.

The blossom is smiling on my apple tree,
And the birds are singing, oh so merrily!
And the sun is shining just for you and me
Hey Ho! It's Spring again.

Couples are walking hand-in-hand,
Most are thinking of a golden band,
It's happening now, all over this land.
Hey Ho! It's Spring again.

DAECCA'S STORY

The longboat wallowed sluggishly in the water, scarcely moving, for the amount of water coming through the damage to the hull was almost at danger level.

It was meant to be rowed by forty men, but with only six men and four women, one of whom was heavily pregnant, together with four children who were trying to bail out the water, it was a losing battle.

They were making their way towards the mouth of a small river that emptied into the Thames that they had been on for the past three days.

Soon after starting from Conberg in Denmark, weeks ago (no one could remember just how many), in company with thirty-two other long ships, illness had hit their boat, and men, women and children had died each day. Whatever cures they had tried, nothing made any effect and when the other crews realised their plight, they pulled away, wishing them joy in the next world.

Eventually they reached the coast of Essex, but wherever they tried to land, they were expelled by their ex-friends and treated as if they were already dead, and were pelted with rocks and stones and at Wivenhoe, one man attacked their long ship with an axe, making several holes in the hull.

The disease that had killed off so many of their company had now stopped spreading and there had been no more deaths for nearly two weeks, but morale was very low.

They moved into the river Thames after a few days, going first to the south side in the hope of a better reception, but the settlers were even more ferocious and they had to move back. All the time their boat was filling with water and getting heavier and the wind changed direction and blew against them.

Daecca cried out that they could not last much longer and had to reach land before the boat sank and the boat beached just near the mouth of a small river. For the first time in over a week, all managed to step onto dry land. Taking only the sail and some fishing lines, the women cast out the lines as the men built a shelter with the sail and they made a fire to dry themselves and their clothes.

Backor, who had been the navigator, woke first in the morning, just as dawn was breaking. Smelling a strong rancid smell, for a minute or two he wondered from where it came, then he knew it was marsh gas! He knew this would not be uncommon in marsh beside rivers, but he also knew what that gas could do. He had to be quick before they were all overpowered!

He called out as loud as he was able, waking the others within seconds and shaking those who would rather just turn over. They ran and Daecca made towards the woods that were about a mile away, trying to go as fast as possible being forced to go further westward than he wanted by the need to find a solid path through the marsh. The children were crying and the women complaining that they were still tired and Daecca sank to his knees a couple of times, and needed to be pulled out by the other men.

Eventually all reached the tree line. And walking a little further, found a good clearing which was large enough so that at least they could easily see anybody approaching. They sank to the ground, raising a prayer to the skies, but most were asleep before it was finished.

Finally, when they awoke late the next morning, they saw the sun shining on a very pleasant valley, with a stream running through it and woods on three sides, far enough away to be safe but not too far for gathering wood, nuts, and berries and many other things useful to them. Snares were set in no time and two men went off into the woods seeking game for they wanted to fill their cooking pots as soon as they were rescued from the boat. Daecca remained resting longer to recover, for he had seen the deer and rabbits at the edge of the woods and thought he had time and they would still not go hungry.

During the next few days, their labour was divided between building the camp and going back to the boat that was stuck in the mud. They were salvaging as much as possible for there remained many clothes and tools from the people who had died on the boat journey. On the sixth day one woman said she thought she'd seen someone looking at them from the edge of the woods, but the men's investigations found nothing. But they then decided to leave a person on lookout after that.

Two days later, they found that a deer had fallen into a pit dug as part of their camp's defense. That night, they were able to feast well, especially as that day Daecca's son was born! With mother and baby extremely healthy, Daecca was well pleased with this new life. But the stranger appeared again which worried them but then they found he had left half a sheep in the space between the trees and their camp. He had also left two bows and a dozen arrows so they considered he came in peace.

Breaking their fast just after dawn the next morning, the stranger came again bringing with him two women and another male and they all held out their hands showing that no weapons were carried. Both sides now made efforts to talk to each other but they had to convert to sign language.

The newcomers clearly indicated that they wanted to join with them, as they had been wandering alone for weeks as their lands had been taken from them by the King's men so he could use it as a hunting ground. Daecca was willing for the newcomers to join them provided they kept to their own sleeping places until they had proved themselves.

With extra hands the camp was soon built and as three cows and several sheep were "found" in the woods, the children could drink milk for the first time in many months.

The firm hand of Daecca ruled the camp but he was always fair in his decisions and in time more people came to join them. Each was allocated work to suit their strengths, woodmen, hunters, farmers and so on.

When the first trees were cut down, men carved fertility symbols from wood and these were planted in the ground to help the crops to grow. Those symbols resembled little men and prayers were said as they were planted.

After one of the newcomer's had been with the group for a few weeks he said he was very happy to be at Daecca's hamlet and from then on that name stuck...

Months and years went by, there were good and bad seasons but the camp prospered and Daecca and his small group of headmen, prudently stored grain and food and they were all fed throughout the winter maintaining their survival.

But things that simple couldn't last, just when the settlement was established, a crime took place which upset everyone and everything.

It began when Vorgan, who was only twenty years old and had been with them just a few months, fell in love with the wife of one of the herdsmen. Unfortunately, she was not averse to his advances and soon became pregnant and when her condition could not be denied, the truth came out. Seeking to resolve the matter, Daecca called the headmen together.

The herdsman forgave his wife, admitting he was partly at fault as she had been left alone for long periods. Daecca decreed that Vorgan must forfeit half of his goods and leave the settlement forever but as he finished speaking, Vorgan rose up, and before he could be stopped ran to Daecca and stabbed him in the heart. He fell to the ground as the blood poured from the wound and although many the men rushed to his aid there was nothing they could do. Daecca died in their arms as the rest of the men stopped Vorgan escaping and in their anguish, hacked him to pieces.

People came from many miles around to attend the funeral pyre of Daecca for he was much revered for his fairness although strict rule of his domain. The feasting and celebration of his life lasted for many days.

Eventually, a new leader was elected for the hamlet, but it was never the same as in the day of Daecca...

HOTFOOT

I've been here before, well not exactly where I am now, but in Egypt, which I fell in love with a few years ago. I've 'done' all the usual tourist attractions but what fascinates me the most is that if you travelled to the end of the main road through most villages, and usually it was the only road, it always ended in sand.

Sand, sand, sand - in any direction, as far as the eye could see, with patterns of light on the dunes, at different times of the day, giving vistas worthy of any art gallery. The sheer vastness and silence gave me new perspectives on the world.

I had travelled out to Egypt with a party of archaeologists but soon left them at the station for searching old ruins is not really my cup of tea.

Hiring a car in Egypt can be a bit of a gamble, especially in the small villages where I go, there you often need luck to drive it out of the garage. So, usually I hire a four-wheel drive vehicle in Cairo, right at the start of my holiday.

On this holiday, on the last day, I drove a few miles into the desert to enjoy a final look before going back to Cairo and home but three miles along the track, I noticed the temperature gauge on the dashboard had risen onto the red section. I stopped and looking under the bonnet, I soon found the cause and fixed it. Now, I needed the engine to cool before driving back so I waited and tried to sleep. Worried that I might not get back in time, sleep would not come and I sat and stared out at the dunes before me...

Suddenly, there was a tiny speck on the horizon that was getting rapidly bigger. Focusing my binoculars, I saw a person on a camel coming straight towards me at full gallop. As the image drew nearer, I could see that the rider was a woman wearing a broad-brimmed hat that hid her face and a white shirt with a black skirt covering most of her legs but I could clearly see her feet and they were enclosed in the most hideous multi-coloured sandals.

Although my motor's engine was now cool something wouldn't let me leave until I had met the woman, so I waited for her to come to me.

Getting out of the motor, I started to walk towards her. She seemed to be wearing sunglasses but as she came nearer, I realised with horror, that the two round, dark spaces that I thought were sunglass lens were in fact the empty eye sockets of a skeleton! It also became clear that her clothes were just hanging on her bones, which were without any movement, as you would expect from the motion of the camel.

I froze with shock, but then as the camel and rider came abreast of where I was standing, I put out my hand to grab the rope hanging from the camel's mouth. But there was nothing to hold, so I raised my hand further, making to grab the bridle but my hand went straight through the camel's head...

I don't know how I covered that distance back to the motor and I can't remember starting the engine, nor any of the journey back to my digs. I only remember rushing to open the whisky bottle when I got there and taking an almighty swig before throwing myself onto the bed, shaking and sweating. It was sometime before I remembered I needed to get to Cairo and the airport, to catch my flight home, so quickly gathering all my clothes, camera and things everything got thrown into my holdalls and I got going. The journey to Cairo was quicker than usual but when I arrived there was a message waiting. It said that Annabel, one of the archaeologists who had travelled out from England with our party on the plane, had not arrived from the hotel and asked that as I was the only one who still had a car, would I go and pick her up?

I worked it out that if I hurried, I just had enough time to get there and back, so thinking that doing this would help to take my mind off the recent happenings, I left and as I drove, I thought about the coming hours when I would soon be home in my little flat in London and I thought how after a couple of hours sleep, I would get ready and go out to meet my mates at the Black Bull and tell them about all my experiences.

Approaching the meeting place with Annabel, I passed a string of camels which reminded me of that morning so that I began again to shake. Once the camels had passed I began to settle my nerves but was brought to stop again by a large crowd milling about in the road, all jabbering excitedly. A policeman seemed to be searching for something on the ground and curious I asked him what was the problem "Oh, some silly British tourist woman has been knocked down and killed as she tried to cross the road wearing these stupid things" he said, as he pulled out from his bag a pair of hideous multi-coloured sandals...

...I was told by my doctor the other day, that if I keep taking the tablets, I might be out in a month or so and electric shock treatment had been necessary to eradicate the memory of my LAST holiday in Egypt.

I am hoping someone kept up with the rent on my flat these months that I've been away, as I will need somewhere to relax when I am finally allowed home.

If I take a holiday next year, I think it will be a week in the Lake District, hopefully there I will find solitude that I still crave!

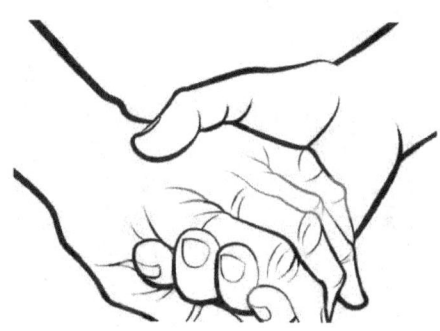

If you want to make a dream, then make a dream for two,
Then maybe very soon, you'll meet somebody who,
Will want to take you by the hand, and help you understand
That he would want to share your dream with you.
So he'll say...

If you'll let me hold your hand, I'll sing to you.
And if the words should win your heart, I'll bring to you,
A love so strong and true, that is waiting here for you,
So, please let me hold your hand,
And sing to you.

We were strolling through the park, and as it started to get dark,
I tried to kiss you.
Yes, kiss you.
You said it was much too soon, so I waited for the moon,
And then I kissed you.
Yes, I kissed you.
I took you in my arms, admired all your charms,
you spoke of all your dreams and I told you of my schemes,
and under the moonlit sky above we finally spoke of love,
Then, YOU kissed me.

Many years have been and gone, but love just carried on,
because I kissed you,
and you kissed me.
Between the tears and all the fun, we had a daughter and a son,
because you kissed me,
and I kissed you.
You polished up your charms, helped me with my schemes, and twixt all these
many things we tried to fulfil our dreams.
Now sometimes for a lark, you push my wheelchair through the park,
and you kiss me,
and I kiss you.

OUT IN THE COLD

I'm cold, I don't think I've ever been as cold as this and it's not even winter. That was over months ago.

Finding this large cardboard box is something I am getting more pleased about as time passes, and I wrap myself in it closer and closer. The wind has changed direction, coming from the east straight into this doorway but I can't move from here and I expect every doorway in the vicinity is full and has been for some time.

I'm trying to sleep now, but the cold is getting into my bones. It doesn't help to turn over as these flagstones seem as cold wherever my body touches. I doze for a while, thinking two hours have passed, but when I look at my watch it has been only twenty minutes. To tire my brain, I try to think of something complicated, but I become more wide awake because I can't find any answers.

The times tables that I learnt at school appear to work, and I doze before I finish them but half asleep, I begin to turn over, for it was too painful when my elbow came into contact with the edge of the step. I am awake again.

The night drags on, traffic noises nearly die away, except for the occasional motorcyclist who revels in making as much noise as possible. Peace and quiet reign at last, and that word brings on the drizzle which lasts the rest of the night.

I pull my hood further over my head, trying to keep dry and I pondered on the reasons that have brought me to this. I regret the path I have taken and wish I had more will power to say no to the temptation.

I've finished the flask of coffee bought in the little cafe hours ago and what with the cold and rain, I wish I had put some brandy, or something similar in it. Now it is four a.m. and I feel low, then suddenly I am startled by the sound of a bad tempered taxi driver using his horn to bully the driver in front. I panic, frantically looking at my watch to find it is just a little after seven o'clock and know that I and three others sharing this doorway have plenty of time before we have to get out of the way.

Quietly, after brushing my hair and putting on lipstick, I roll up my sleeping bag, deflate my air pillow and tying them up I succeed in not waking anyone. I am ready and whilst watching the slow build-up of traffic I start to run through just what I have decided to do when we are finally made to move. Just after seven-thirty, two or three people come to the inside of the glass doors and stare at us; two of my 'bedfellows' are still sleeping.

At ten to eight, a police car pulls into the curb and a large sergeant comes over to tell us to get back from the door. All four of us start to argue with him and get him confused until it is time for the doors to open at eight o'clock. Then we move so fast we nearly knock the men inside down. I know my route like the back of my hand, up the escalator, turn right straight into the ladies coat department...and there it is, a beautiful five hundred pound fur coat on sale for fifty pounds!

I make a grab for it and feeling good because I am yards ahead of everyone else I lunged towards it but my foot slips on the edge of the stand and I fall headfirst.

The next thing I remember is I am walking along the high street wearing the coat, but it is a misty dream, soon dispelled by the thumping headache in a band around my head. The band turns out to be a bandage holding a very large dressing.

I realise that I am in bed but these sounds and smells are not the ones I'm used to at home. My fur coat has turned into a slightly faded hospital gown with not enough tapes across the back, to protect my dignity, which I find distressing when I am finally allowed to get out of bed.

A couple of weeks later I went back to the store to thank the first aiders for looking after me and stemming the blood from my forehead. I will have a scar for a long time, I'm told - I think I will get one of those Russian fur hats to cover it... but I have decided to sleep on that idea!

ALICE PARDUE – A SPIRIT OF VALENCE HOUSE

I approached Valence House from across the park, wanting to take it in slowly as it had been many years since I had been here. Looking back over the park, I could see the snow that had been falling nearly all day, laying like a blanket covering everything without a blemish. It was just beginning to glisten as the air started to freeze.

I glanced at the moat and thought that if the ice got any thicker its purpose would be lost. The lights were on in the house as dusk was falling and they cast a golden glow onto the snow. As I moved away, the door opened and five or six people came out, slipping and sliding and trying to hold each other up. Now, I was too far away to hear just what they were saying, I only heard giggling and the word Christmas.

Coming into the shadow of a strange building it seemed, at first to have no roof, and as I marvelled at the amount of glass on the front of it I skirted around a strange brown object covered in snow - so much had changed since my last visit.

I drifted slowly over to the side of the house, passing through the kitchen on my way and then out into the garden, my favourite place, where I spent so many happy hours picking herbs and tending the vegetables.

Yes, I enjoyed a great deal of pleasure there, especially 'helping' Samuel the junior gardener. That was why I was dismissed by Mr. Coote from my job as kitchen maid. As expected, Samuel had left earlier, without having time to see me.

I had nowhere to go at such short notice and in weather just as bad as it is today, I went to sit in the garden. I was found there the following morning, frozen stiff. That was Christmas Eve 1609, but I will come back again - I have to come back, in the hope of seeing Samuel again and to tell him I'm sorry.

I once made a table
That's when I was able,
I wanted to make one to suit me.
I outlined it, designed it
And slowly I refined it
'til I saw what I wanted to see......

I sought out some wood,
The very best that I could,
(Turned out to be nice mahogany)
I planed it, I sawed it
I found a drill and bored it,
And sanded as fine as it could be.

I squared it, I screwed it,
Clamped it, and glued it
And did the dowels so that you couldn't see
I stained it, then polished
To a nearly perfect finish.
And I saw what I wanted to see.......

When I finished that there table,
And was finally able
To see what I wanted to see,
I knew t'was made of wood,
And believe it I should,
But I'm sure it was really made OF ME.

The sun had just set and the light was beginning to fade as I started out on my usual jaunt around town. It was my time of day and year, with Autumn's slightly lower temperatures and softer lighting.

The streets were deserted, smoke curled lazily from the chimneys of the houses, as wives and mothers cooked their family's evening meal; husbands, tired out after their long day at work, and children, who also had to do a share of the work were waiting patiently for the treat to come.

As yet, very few lights had appeared in the windows for gas was used sparingly. Not many could afford to keep lights on for the whole evening even though the tall buildings each side of the road, kept the houses in almost perpetual shadow.

Wandering from road to road, I glanced into the shop windows, and for that matter, any other windows but most of the shops were empty. The tearooms on the corner, where I had taken my first date, with the menus chalked on the board at the back which were still partly readable had only the remains of the counter and tables, disappearing gradually under layers of dust. Other shops still in business, looked sad, and greatly in need of a coat of paint.

I pursued a zigzag course through the maze of narrow passages and alleyways that filled the area. I was not in any hurry, as time did not mean much anymore, I only had a vague plan to reach the other side of town, where the theatre was at some time.

As I turned the next corner, I nearly collided with a "VISION"! That is the only word that came into my mind when I saw the most beautiful woman I had ever seen. She passed me without smiling, for that was the "done" thing at that time. But I followed her, studying her fair hair, upswept in the latest fashion with not a hair out of place, and no sign of a pin or clip to hold it in shape.

Her neck was unblemished and creamy coloured in contrast with the black of the short jacket she wore, which clung so closely to the shape of her figure, and the skirt of her dress hung in soft folds to a hemline so level, it looked almost sculptured.

She seemed to float smoothly as we progressed and by the time I had taken this in, we had reached the road alongside the theatre and the entrance in the main road, away to our left. She stepped back from the curb, keeping as far as possible from the horse and cart that was passing, and I expected her to turn left. I was surprised when she went directly across, for there was no pavement on that side, then surprise turned to shock as without hesitation she moved straight through the wall.

Even more shocking, was that I had almost forgotten my own newly acquired spiritual state, until I found myself following her and after I passed through the wall I came into an almost dark room. The only sign of the "vision" was a slowly closing door in the corner, but in less than a second, I was through that door, and immediately knew where I was...

In the centre was the scrubbed wooden table with the thick leather straps fixed to the sides and the strange tools hanging on hooks on the wall. Surely, this is the place where they had tried and failed to repair the hole in my head after the horse had kicked me – only a week ago.

I was in the middle of the theatre, and she was there, wearing a very white coat and apron, washing her hands at the sink.

'Me thinks', said the Bard, as he strode down the lane,
'I can't find a rhyme for percussion,
I'll ask all my friends when I get to the end
And offer it up for discussion'.

'When we're all at our ease and say what we please
And sometimes our sessions get bawdy,
but our barmaid, young Mary gets all airy-fairy
and boxes our ears when we're nawdey'.

"Happy Days"
Frank and Evelyn Beale

The Archives & Local Studies Centre at Valence House Museum in the London Borough of Barking & Dagenham is the source and inspiration for many local heritage projects. When volunteers working there wish to develop and expand topics of significant local historical interest they are encouraged with the generous support of the professional staff.

This publication is the original work of Frank Beale a volunteer at Valence House since 2009. His memories are a unique reflection of his life spent in Dagenham. We are pleased to be able to publish these memories and his stories in his 92nd year. He is still active as a volunteer often in the capacity of an elder statesman and all the staff and volunteers value his friendship.

Previous Valence House Publications
Fanshawe's Indian Summer (978-1-911391-05-0)
Danger Over Dagenham (978-1-911391-06-7)
Abyssinia 1868 Last Great Expedition of Queen Victoria's Army
(978-1-911391-02-9)
Sebastopol to Dagenham (978-1-911391-02-9)
A History of Dagenham (978-1-911391-03-6)
The Life of Sir Richard Fanshawe (978-1-911391-00-5)
The Death of the 'Dukes' (978-1-911391-99-9)

www.ingramcontent.com/pod-product-compliance
Lightning Source LLC
Chambersburg PA
CBHW050719090526
44588CB00014B/2338